Thank You My Friend

You can personalize this book for your Friend!

Find a special photograph of you!
Simply tape your photo on the corners and place over the photo on this page.
Make sure that your photo shows through the window of the book's front cover.

Thank You,
My Friend

*No distance of place or lapse of time can lessen
the friendship of those who are thoroughly
persuaded of each other's worth.*

ROBERT SOUTHEY

Thank You, My Friend

A Keepsake in Celebration of Friendship

BLUE SKY INK

Brentwood, Tennessee

Thank You, My Friend

Copyright © 2004 GRQ, Inc.

ISBN 1-59475-006-8

Published by Blue Sky Ink

Brentwood, Tennessee.

Editor: Lila Empson

Writer: Phillip H. Barnhart

Cover and text design: Diane Whisner

04 05 06   4 3 2

*To have a friend is one
of the sweetest gifts that life
can bring.*

AMY ROBERTSON BROWN

*May the LORD keep watch between you and me
when we are away from each other.*

GENESIS 31:49 NIV

Introduction

My friend, when I take account of the valuables I most treasure, you are one of them. You are there for me when I wonder if anyone will be. You stand tall with me when I feel inadequate and lift me to my feet when I've forgotten how to walk. You love me even when you don't understand me. Our friendship is a deep well from which I drink.

Sometimes I wonder what I would be if you had not come into my life. Would I be as confident? Would I be as secure? Would I be as successful? Would I be as close to God?

You assess me by my desires and intentions. You tell me the truth. You see in me things I do not see in myself.

Thank you, my friend.

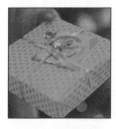

Two are better than one. . . .
For if they fall, one will lift
up the other.

ECCLESIASTES 4:9–10 NRSV

*If instead of a gem, or
even a flower, we should
cast the gift of a loving
thought into the heart of
a friend, that would be
giving as the angels give.*

GEORGE MACDONALD

Treat your friends as you do your pictures, and place them in the best light.

JENNIE JEROME CHURCHILL

Real friends will share even a strawberry.

SLOVAKIAN PROVERB

*The first rule for friendship
is to be a friend, to be
open, natural, interested;
the second rule is to take
time for friendship.*

Nels F. S. Ferre

*Love must be completely sincere. Hate
what is evil, hold on to what is good.
Love one another warmly as
Christians, and be eager to show
respect for one another. Work hard and
do not be lazy. Serve the Lord with a
heart full of devotion.*

ROMANS 12:9–11 GNT

The great joy of our friendship is that we both deeply feel it is Jesus who has brought us together.

HENRI J. M. NOUWEN

If you haven't learned the meaning of friendship, you really haven't learned anything.

MUHAMMAD ALI

One Friend
Remembers . . .

I remember when I made that mistake and wondered if I would ever get over it. One of my friends never did get over it. When he sees me, he hangs his head and quickly finds the other side of the street. The remembrance of what I did is too much for him

But you were never that way. When I made that mistake, you saw right through me but somehow still enjoyed the view. You knew what I had done, but that is not all you remembered about me.

You were more interested in where I was going than in where I had been. Your friendship gave me hope. As you walked with me, doors opened everywhere.

*The LORD has done great things for us,
and we are filled with joy.*

PSALM 126:3 NIV

*Friends don't count in fair weather. It is
when trouble comes that friends count.*

HARRY TRUMAN

*Our ancestors regarded
friendship as something that
raised us almost above humanity.
This love, free from instinct, free
from all duties but those which
love has freely assumed, almost
wholly free from jealousy,
without qualification from the
need to be needed, is eminently
spiritual. It is the sort of love one
can imagine between angels.*

C. S. LEWIS

Under the magnetism of friendship the modest person becomes bold; the shy, confident; the lazy, active; the impetuous, prudent and peaceful.

WILLIAM THACKERAY

Hold a true friend with both your hands.

NIGERIAN PROVERB

Beloved, I pray that in all respects you may prosper and be in good health, just as your soul prospers.

3 JOHN 1:2 NASB

*One loyal friend is worth
ten thousand relatives.*

EURIPIDES

*May the Lord continually bless you with
heaven's blessings as well as with human joys.*

PSALM 128:5 TLB

*Love one another the way I loved you.
This is the very best way to love.
Put your life on the line for your friends.*

JOHN 15:12–13 THE MESSAGE

*Jesus is the never ending
horizon of infinite friendship
we journey into through the
port of each one we meet.*

ERNEST LARSON

Friendships are fragile, and require as much care in handling as other fragile and precious possessions.

RALPH S. BOURNE

Did You Know?

*I*n 1960, Jack Twyman, star forward for the Cincinnati Royals professional basketball team, was given the Sportsmanship Brotherhood plaque in recognition of his having taken care of his retired teammate Maurice Stokes after he was stricken with encephalitis in 1958. The devoted friendship between those two had a tremendous impact on behalf of racial harmony in sports.

*Your words have supported
those who were stumbling,
and you have made firm the
feeble knees.*

JOB 4:4 NRSV

The next time I have the urge to speak negatively or rudely to you, I'll swallow and be silent. Loving you doesn't give me license for rudeness.

LEO BUSCAGLIA

I always felt that the high privilege, relief, and comfort of friendship was that one had to explain nothing.

KATHERINE MANSFIELD

Robbing life of friendship is like robbing the world of the sun.

CICERO

The source of friendship is God. Once we establish that fundamental relationship, human friends come naturally, for people migrate toward the wholesomeness God engenders.

DONALD E. DEMARAY

*The people you have great empathy with are seldom
conveniently located nearby. Some are, but most are
scattered far and wide. You see them too seldom. But
you can always pick up right where you left off. You
know who they are. They know who you are. No
reintroductions are required.*

JOHN D. MACDONALD

True friendship is like sound health; the value of it is seldom known until it is lost.

CHARLES CALEB COLTON

We all take different paths in life, but no matter where we go, we take a little of each other everywhere.

TIM MCGRAW

Those who stepped on us in the past may remain standing there until someone on our side helps us pull them off. Time will not heal nor reactivate our will to live. Only true love can make it up to us. We must find a friend who will pick this burden off our backs, this oppressive reminiscence we cannot quite detect or move alone. Friends must undo what enemies did.

DAVID A. REDDING

Survival Tip

Five Ways to Friendship:

1. Be the first to make up after a quarrel; do not wait for your friend to apologize.

2. Keep secrets; never leave room for your friend to lose confidence in you.

3. Make a habit of visiting people who are lonely.

4. Do not allow letters to go unanswered, or phone calls unreturned.

5. Take the initiative; make the first move toward friendship.

*A friend loves at all times,
and kinsfolk are born to
share adversity.*

PROVERBS 17:17 NRSV

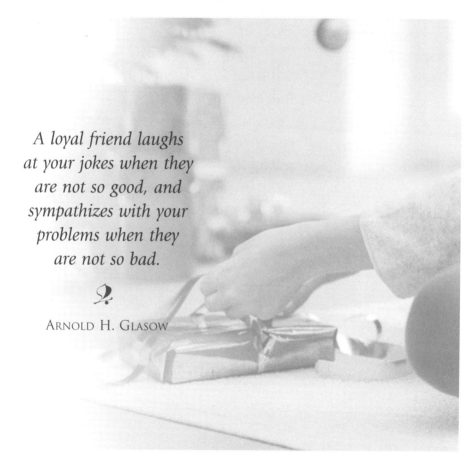

*A loyal friend laughs
at your jokes when they
are not so good, and
sympathizes with your
problems when they
are not so bad.*

ARNOLD H. GLASOW

*Friendship is a single soul
dwelling in two bodies.*

ARISTOTLE

*Life is partly what we make it,
and partly what it is made by the
friends we choose.*

TEHYI HSIEH

*Even the cops are with
you when you are right;
friends have to be with
you when you are wrong.*

ADELA ROGERS ST. JOHN

*A friend is one to whom we may pour
out the contents of our hearts, chaff
and grain together, knowing that the
gentlest of hands will sift it, keep what
is worth keeping, and with a breath of
kindness blow the rest away.*

ARABIAN DEFINITION

Friends On and Off the Court

Rick bounced the ball with one eye on the clock and the other on his best friend, Norm. He caught Norm's eye and rifled a pass to him. Norm gave a head fake, stepped back, drove to the basket, and dunked the ball as the final buzzer sounded. They had won the state high school basketball championship.

The road to victory began when, at age seven, Rick and Norm first played basketball together for their church. They had played basketball and gone to church together eleven years. They were friends on and off the court.

The best place to stand with your friends is on the promises of God.

*Some friends play at friendship
but a true friend sticks closer than
one's nearest kin.*

PROVERBS 18:24 NRSV

*You can make more friends
in two months by becoming
interested in other people
than you can in two years
by trying to get other people
interested in you.*

DALE CARNEGIE

*The difference between men friends and
women friends is men tend to do things
together while women tend just to be together.*

ART JAHNKE

*If Barbie is so popular, why do
you have to buy her friends?*

BUMPER STICKER

True friendship must be based on mutual trust.

JOHN LeCARRE

*I give you a new commandment,
that you love one another. Just as I
have loved you, you also should love
one another. By this everyone will
know that you are my disciples, if
you have love for one another.*

JOHN 13:34–35 NRSV

Everyone hears what you say.
Friends listen to what you say. Best
friends listen to what you don't say.

AUTHOR UNKNOWN

I'll lean on you and you lean on
me and we'll be okay.

DAVE MATTHEWS BAND

One Friend Remembers...

I remember when my husband was in the hospital and you came by every day. After you got off work, on Saturday mornings, Sundays after church. You brought cards of encouragement. You arranged flowers you had picked, and placed them by the bed. Once you sneaked in Harmon's favorite candy bar. You were so good to my husband, but that's not what I remember most. I remember most the way you always inquired about how I felt. How was I coping with Harmon's condition? Was I jeopardizing my job by being at the hospital so much? Was I able to pray? You were concerned about me. A friend calculates the need in your heart and meets it.

*Pay everything you owe. But you can never
pay back all the love you owe each other.
Those who love others have done
everything the law requires.*

ROMANS 13:8 NIrV

*If you should die before me, ask if you
could bring a friend.*

STONE TEMPLE PILOTS

We need someone to believe in us. If we do well, we want our work commended and our faith corroborated. The individual who thinks well of you, who keeps focused on your good qualities, and does not look for flaws, is your friend. Who is my friend? I'll tell you. My friend is the one who recognizes the good in me.

ELBERT HUBBARD

God who created more than one hundred
thousand galaxies is our friend.

P. BRANDT

May the hinges of friendship
never grow rusty.

IRISH BLESSING

*You must make allowance for
each other's faults and forgive
the person who offends you.
Remember, the Lord forgave
you, so you must forgive others.*

COLOSSIANS 3:13 NLT

To know someone here or there with whom you feel there is an understanding in spite of distances or thoughts unexpressed, that can make of this earth a garden.

JOHANN GOETHE

49

*When the day of Pentecost had come,
they were all together in one place.*

ACTS 2:1 NRSV

*There is . . . one Lord, one faith, one
baptism, one God and Father of all.*

EPHESIANS 4:4 NIV

*Dear friends, no matter
how we find them, are
as essential as breathing
in and breathing out.*

LOIS WYSE

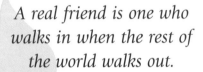

A real friend is one who walks in when the rest of the world walks out.

AUTHOR UNKNOWN

Did You Know?

*I*n the movie *Beaches*, Hillary and CC have been friends since childhood. The bond they forged then grew stronger over the years, and each would do anything for the other. Now Hillary is dying and CC has come to be with her. As she offers her friend encouragement and comforts her the best she can, the movie's musical theme is heard in the background—"You are the wind beneath my wings."

*Practice loving each
other, for love comes
from God and those
who are loving and
kind show that they are
children of God.*

1 JOHN 4:7 TLB

*Real friends are those who,
when you feel you've made a
fool of yourself, don't think
you've done a permanent job.*

AUTHOR UNKNOWN

We must love our friends as true amateurs love paintings; they have their eyes perpetually fixed on the fine parts, and see no others.

MADAME D'EPINAY

Mutuality is the stuff of existence. Selfhood is not created in a closet but in a contact.

DAVID O. WOODYARD

I love the Lord and therefore
I love you, my friend.

BETSY EDWARDS

Closely related to the burning of chaff out of us is the galvanizing of our relationships by the fire of the Holy Spirit. Welding takes white-fire. So do deep, inseparable relationships. The fire in my heart coupled with the fire in yours makes us one.

Lloyd John Ogilvie

To love another person is to see the face of God.

JEAN VAL JEAN

The easiest kind of relationship for me is with ten thousand people. The hardest is with one.

JOAN BAEZ

*To know the Lord Jesus
involves not only a vertical
dimension with the living God
but also horizontal relationships within the family of
God. A beautiful symmetry
results. By abiding in Christ,
I am able to love my fellow
believers. By loving them,
I abide more deeply in my
Father's love.*

LEE STROBEL

Survival Tip

How to Grow a Friendship:

- I won't stand in your way.
- I won't put my problems on you.
- I don't always have to be right.
- I don't always have to run the show.
- I don't have to be perfect, nor do you.
- I can give up wanting to change you.
- I don't need to place blame.
- I can give up unrealistic expectations.

I thank my God upon every remembrance of you.

PHILIPPIANS 1:3 KJV

*I guess I'd rather be famous
than infamous, but about all
that really impresses me is
human kindness and warm
relationships with good friends.*

ROBERT FROST

Sometimes our light goes out but is blown into flame by an encounter with another human being.

ALBERT SCHWEITZER

I have learned that it is not what you have in your life but who you have in your life that counts.

AUTHOR UNKNOWN

Living depends on loving and loving depends on knowing and knowing depends on risking.

MAXIE DUNNAM

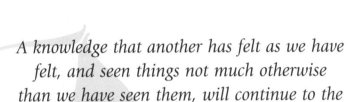

A knowledge that another has felt as we have felt, and seen things not much otherwise than we have seen them, will continue to the end to be one of life's choicest blessings.

ROBERT LOUIS STEVENSON

Loving God Together

The church was full as Hattie and Talitha stepped to the pulpit. Talitha put her arm around Hattie as they picked up the microphones. For thirty minutes, they raised their voices in praise to God. When they finished, the audience exploded in thanksgiving while mother and daughter embraced in a merger of love and affection.

Hattie and Talitha looked so much alike people thought they were twins instead of mother and daughter. They were the closest of friends who often talked late into the night like a couple of sorority sisters. Above all, Hattie and Talitha loved God and spent every minute they could singing his praises. The best recipe for a good home is for everyone in your family to love the Lord.

May the Lord continually bless you with heaven's blessings as well as with human joys.

PSALM 128:5 TLB

*We have not made ourselves;
we are the gift of the living
God to one another.*

REINE DUELL BETHANY

*God's friendship is the unexpected joy we find
when we reach his outstretched hand.*

JANET L. WEAVER SMITH

*The opportunity to practice friendship presents
itself every time you meet a human being.*

JANE WYMAN

As the pressures of life intensify, sometimes the difference between going after a dream and remaining passive is having someone say, "I believe in you."

GARY SMALLEY

*Ever since I heard of your faith in
the Lord Jesus and your love for all
of God's people, I have not stopped
giving thanks to God for you. I
remember you in my prayers.*

EPHESIANS 1:15–16 GNT

I love getting mail. Just the fact that someone licked a stamp for you is very reassuring.

THOMAS MAGNUM

Everyone has an invisible sign hanging from their neck saying, "Make me feel important."

MARY KAY

One Friend Remembers...

I remember when I was wiped out because I didn't get that promotion. I thought I had it all wrapped up, but someone else got it.

I was writing a letter of resignation when you came into my cubicle. You asked me what I was doing, and I gave you the letter to read. You read it, tore it into little pieces, and walked away.

For days I was angry with you. But I never rewrote the letter. What I perceived as your rash act gave me time to think things over. I had a good job, was still young, and would get other chances. I thanked God you had done what you did.

*Be kind and compassionate to one
another, forgiving each other, just as
in Christ God forgave you.*

EPHESIANS 4:32 NIV

*Kind words are jewels that live in the heart
and soul and remain as blessed memories
years after they have been spoken.*

MARVEA JOHNSON

What shall I bestow upon a friend?
Fleeting moments of silent blessings; trust
in tomorrow, which is life's hardest task;
faith that each new dawn brings day-
light's golden pathway to the ever-open
door; and a belief that God will be with
them though all others go their way.

LEA PALMER

When you meet a friend, touch that person. You might touch the God who appears between you.

CARLYLE MARNEY

Happiness is a perfume you cannot pour on others without getting a few drops on yourself.

LOUIS MANN

God blesses those who are merciful,
for they will be shown mercy.

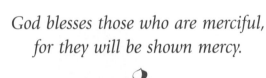

MATTHEW 5:7 NLT

*I've learned that just
one person saying to
me, "You've made my
day!" makes my day.*

ANDY ROONEY

*I will open the windows of heaven for you
and pour out a blessing so great you won't
have room enough to take it in!*

MALACHI 3:10 TLB

*May the Lord make your love increase and
overflow for each other and for everyone
else, just as ours does for you.*

1 THESSALONIANS 3:12 NIV

I can live for two months
on a good compliment.

MARK TWAIN

Turn to the miracle next to you.

HAL EDWARDS

Did You Know?

*D*id you know that more than fifty percent of the people in the world have never received or made a telephone call?

Did you know "I am" is the shortest complete sentence in the English language?

Did you know that, like fingerprints, everyone's tongue print is different?

Did you know that people say "Bless you" when you sneeze because, when you sneeze, your heart stops for a millisecond?

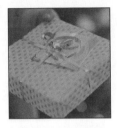

*Pleasant words are a
honeycomb, sweet to the soul
and healing to the bones.*

PROVERBS 16:24 NIV

God's heart is the most sensitive and tender of all. No act goes unnoticed, no matter how insignificant or small.

RICHARD J. FOSTER

The friend given you by circumstances
over which you have no control was
God's own gift.

FREDERICK ROBERTSON

My friend shall forever be my friend
and reflect a ray of God to me.

HENRY DAVID THOREAU

A friend understands what you are trying to say, even when your thoughts aren't fitting your words.

ANN D. PARRISH

When personal relationships break down, it is a sure sign there is some rift in one's relationship with God. The deeper the rift, the broader will be the effect on the human level. We "get at" God by getting at those he has made, especially those he has placed close to us. To recognize and submit to that claim is to return to peace and fellowship

ELISABETH ELLIOT

*When you are with a friend, your
heart has come home.*

EMILY FARRAR

Friendship is one of the sweetest joys of life.

CHARLES SPURGEON

Above all, let us never forget that an act of goodness is in itself an act of happiness. It is the flower of a long inner life of joy and contentment; it tells of peaceful hours and days on the sunniest heights of our soul.

MAURICE MAETERLINCK

Survival Tip

*P*aint Friendship:

- Red, the color of passion and love.
- Orange, the color of health and strength.
- Yellow, the color of laughter and warmth.
- Green, the color of life and hope.
- Blue, the color of peace and serenity.
- Indigo, the color of silence and inner peace.
- Purple, the color of royalty and power.

Join them together in a rainbow for today and tomorrow.

God's blessing makes life rich;
nothing we do can improve on God.

PROVERBS 10:22 THE MESSAGE

A friend is a present you give yourself.

Author Unknown

*One of the quickest ways to feel tired
is to suppress your feelings.*

SUE PATTON THOEK

Am I capable of acting better than I feel?

DOUG MESKE

Christian fellowship is living with and for one another responsibly, that is, in love.

REUEL L. HOWE

*I wish you sunshine on your path
and storms to season your journey.
I wish you peace, in the world
where you live and in the smallest
corner of the heart where truth is
kept. More I cannot wish you,
except perhaps love, to make the
rest worthwhile.*

ROBERT A. WARD

Friends Forget and Remember

Two friends walking through the desert had an argument, and one slapped the other. The one who was slapped wrote in the sand: "Today my friend slapped me."

They kept walking until they found an oasis, where they took a swim. The one who had been slapped began to drown, and his friend saved him. He wrote on a stone: "Today my friend saved my life."

Asked to explain, he said, "When a friend hurts us, we should write in the sand where it can be erased. When a friend does something for us, we should engrave it in stone where it can never be erased."

Friends forget and remember in all the right places.

I have loved you even as the Father has loved me. Remain in my love.

JOHN 15:9 NLT

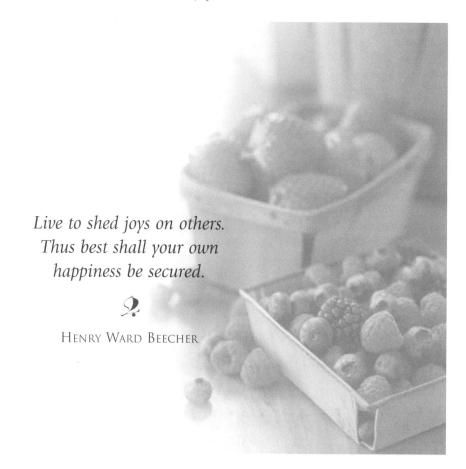

Live to shed joys on others.
Thus best shall your own
happiness be secured.

Henry Ward Beecher

You cannot use your friends
and have them too.

FARMER'S ALMANAC

Happiness comes of the
capacity to feel deeply, to
enjoy simply, to think freely,
to risk life, to be needed.

STORM (MARGARET) JAMESON

All your strength is in union. All your danger is in discord.

HENRY WADSWORTH
LONGFELLOW

*Do not judge, and you will not be
judged; do not condemn, and you will
not be condemned. Forgive, and you
will be forgiven; give and it will be
given to you. A good measure, pressed
down, shaken together, running over,
will be put into your lap.*

LUKE 6:37–38 NRSV

We are more alike than we are unlike.

MAYNARD JACKSON

It is as necessary for the heart to feel
as for the body to be fed.

NAPOLEON BONAPARTE

One Friend
Remembers . . .

I remember your family taking me in as if I had been born to them. My mother had raised me by herself when you all came out of nowhere to embrace and love me. I never knew my dad but, after a while, that didn't make much difference. I didn't know what grandparents were until you started treating me as one of your family. I remember the first time you said, "And this is our granddaughter, Betsy."

You took me to Walt Disneyland. I even had my own suitcase and my own spending money. You never forgot my birthday, and I had most of my parties at your house. You never left me out of anything.

Sometimes, family is where you find it.

*Whenever you stand praying, forgive, if you
have anything against anyone; so that your
Father in heaven may also forgive you.*

MARK 11:25 NRSV

*Let us be grateful to people who make us
happy; they are the charming gardeners
who make our souls blossom.*

MARCEL PROUST

Times of spiritual apathy are the very times when we can do most to prove our love for God, and I have no doubt we bring most joy to his heart when we defy our feelings and act in spite of them.

J. B. PHILLIPS

Joy shared is a double delight, and sorrow shared is half a burden.

It took an artist divine to make your design.

JAMES FORBES

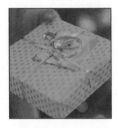

Anyone who gives a lot will succeed.
Anyone who renews others will be renewed.

PROVERBS 11:25 NIrV

In God's wisdom,
He frequently chooses
to meet our needs by
showing His love
toward us through the
hands and hearts
of others.

JACK HAYFORD

The one who sows sparingly will also reap sparingly, and the one who sows bountifully will also reap bountifully.

2 CORINTHIANS 9:6 NRSV

God didn't give us a spirit that makes us weak and fearful. He gave us a spirit that gives us power and love.

2 TIMOTHY 1:7 NIrV

Compassion is about stepping outside of yourself.

JULIE BARR

Only empathy can build the connection needed for healing.

BERNIE S. SIEGEL

Did You Know?

C. S. Lewis and J. R. R. Tolkien were good friends who met together at Oxford at a place called The Eagle and Child in a group named "The Inklings." There they sat around a table, critiquing each other's work. Around that table, such manuscripts as The Chronicles of Narnia and The Lord of the Rings Trilogy took shape. It was also there that Tolkien spoke to Lewis of his Christian faith and the two of them were spiritual pilgrims together.

Don't get tired of doing what is good. Don't get discouraged and give up.

GALATIANS 6:9 NLT

Infinite sadness is not to trust an old friend.

DICK FRANCIS

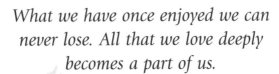

What we have once enjoyed we can never lose. All that we love deeply becomes a part of us.

HELEN KELLER

I thank God far more for friends than for my daily bread, for friendship is the bread of the heart.

MARY MITFORD

If you are blessed with a
sympathetic disposition,
don't waste it on yourself.

BENJAMIN FRANKLIN

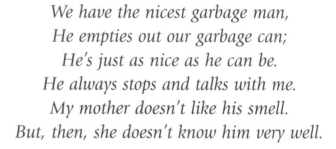

We have the nicest garbage man,
He empties out our garbage can;
He's just as nice as he can be.
He always stops and talks with me.
My mother doesn't like his smell.
But, then, she doesn't know him very well.

G. RAY JORDAN

*One of the finest definitions of sympathy
is your pain in my heart.*

H. E. Luccock

*Hugging is a means of getting two people so
close together they can't see anything wrong
with each other.*

Author Unknown

No man is an island entire of itself; every man is a piece of the Continent, a part of the main. . . . Any man's death diminishes me because I am involved in Mankind; and therefore never send to know for whom the bell tolls; it tolls for thee.

JOHN DONNE

Survival Tip

Seven Blessings of Friendship:

- Slow together is better than fast alone.

- Seeing with four eyes is better than seeing with two eyes.

- Make new friends but keep the old; one is silver and the other is gold.

- Cheerful friends lift you up.

- You and your friends get to see each other change.

- Friendship deepens and sweetens.

- Friends are God's way of taking care of you.

*It is more blessed to give
than to receive.*

Acts 20:35 NLT

I wish you all the joy that you can wish.

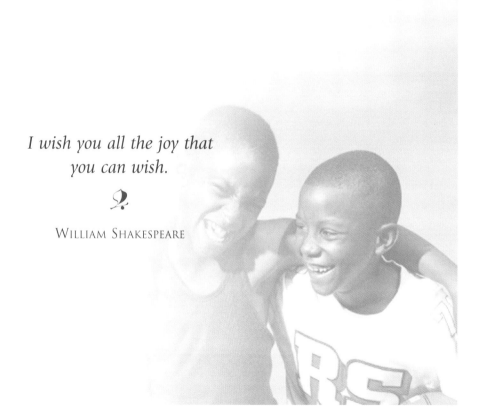

WILLIAM SHAKESPEARE

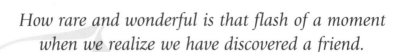

*How rare and wonderful is that flash of a moment
when we realize we have discovered a friend.*

WILLIAM ROTSLER

*Friends are an indispensable part of a meaningful
life. They are the ones who share our burdens and
multiply our blessings.*

BEVERLY LaHAYE

*Think where man's glory
most begins and ends
And say my glory was
I had such friends.*

W. B. YEATS